STAY THE BLEEP OUT OF THE KITCHEN: A QUICK & EASY GUIDE TO LEARN HOW TO NOT SUCK AT PICKLEBALL

Paddle Posh Team
(T.A. Little)

Paddle Posh

PADDLE
P●SH

Copyright © 2024 Paddle Posh

All rights reserved. No part of this book may be reproduced, distributed, or transmitted in any form or by any means, including photocopying, recording, or other electronic or mechanical methods, without the prior written permission of the publisher, except in the case of brief quotations embodied in critical reviews and certain other noncommercial uses permitted by copyright law.

Published in the United States of America by Paddle Posh.
www.paddleposh.com

ISBN: 979-8-218-49995-2

This book is humorous and satirical and is not intended as professional advice. Names, characters, and events depicted in this book are fictitious. Any resemblance to actual persons, living or dead, or actual events is purely coincidental.

The content reflects the author's opinions and experiences with pickleball. Readers should consult official rulebooks or guides for accurate game rules and regulations.

First Edition, 2024
Printed in the United States of America

To all the pickleball fanatics who can't stop talking about the game, even when nobody asked. To the pickleball players who've lost friendships over a kitchen violation, who've sprained things they didn't know could be sprained, and who've proudly worn their pickleball bruises like badges of honor.

To the partners, friends, and family members who put up with the endless stories of epic dinks, devastating smashes, and questionable line calls—this one's for you. May you either join us on the pickleball court or find the patience to listen to us rant about it until you do.

To all the professional and elite pickleball players out there, thank you for being such good sports with this book. Your dedication to the game, incredible skill, and passion for pickleball have not only inspired countless players but have also set the standard for excellence on and off the court. We appreciate your sense of humor as we've added a bit of fun and sass to the mix, and we hope this book brings a smile to your face as much as it does to those who look up to you. Keep smashing it out there, both literally and figuratively!

And finally, to the kitchens everywhere— both the kind you cook in and the kind you stay the bleep out of. Because without you, this game wouldn't be half as fun.

In pickleball, as in life, the secret is knowing when to lob, when to smash, and when to laugh it off.

– TEAM PADDLE POSH

CONTENTS

Title Page

Copyright

Dedication

Epigraph

Introduction

Chapter 1: What the Heck Is Pickleball?	1
Chapter 2: The Basics of Playing	10
Chapter 3: Pickleball Scoring Madness	22
Chapter 4: Pickleball Etiquette (How to Not Be 'That Player')	27
Chapter 5: Pickleball Alter Ego (Don't Be That Person)	31
Chapter 6: Quick Fixes for Your Pickleball Mishaps	38
Chapter 7: How to Practice on Your Own	43
Chapter 8: Recruit, Bribe, or Blackmail: Getting Your People to Play	46
Chapter 9: Winning Without Acting Like a Total Fool (The Art of Good Sportsmanship)	52

Chapter 10: Excuses (For When You're Not Feeling It)	57
Chapter 11: Pre-Game Warm-Up So You Don't Wipe Out	61
Chapter 12: Fun Pickleball Facts	67
Chapter 13: How to Get Better Fast	71
Chapter 14: Post- Game Revovery: Stretch, Brag, and Plot Your Next Victory	75
Chapter 15: Joining a Pickleball Community	79
Chapter 16: Why Pickleball is Here to Stay	84
Chapter 17: Frequently Asked Questions & Confusions	89
Chapter 18: Trading Tennis Whites for Pickleball Smiles	95
Chapter 19: Pickleball Ouchies: Laugh, Cry, and Shake It Off	100
Chapter 20: The Pickleball Glossary: 'Dink' Isn't Just a Weird Noise	104
Chapter 21: Get Out and Play!	112
Congratulations, You've Made it Through the Book!	117
About the Paddle Posh Team	119
For the Love of Pickleball, Share This Book	123

INTRODUCTION

WELCOME TO THE PICKLEBALL MADNESS, YOU MAGNIFICENT PICKLEBALLERS (OR SOON-TO-BE)

Well, look who decided to embrace the chaos that is pickleball finally. Welcome, brave soul. You're about to dive headfirst into the wild, addictive, and slightly unhinged world of pickleball. Yeah, you read that right, pickleball. The sport you never knew you needed but somehow, you can't imagine living without.

This book is your no-B.S.., laugh-out-loud guide to conquering the court and maybe, just maybe, becoming the kind of player who doesn't embarrass themselves in front of their neighbors. We're here to slap you with the cold, hard truths of pickleball, like why you need to stay the bleep out of the kitchen (and no, we're not talking about burning dinner). We're here to make sure you don't suck at this game, and if you do, at least you'll have a good laugh about it.

Whether you're here to improve your game, get a few laughs, or just because someone *ahem* strongly suggested you needed to learn the rules, we've got you covered. Grab your paddle, put on your game face (or your best "I have no idea what I'm doing" expression), and get ready to laugh, learn, and maybe even dominate the court.

So, why should you read this book (or buy it for *that person* who really, really needs it)?

Here's the lowdown:

- **Cut Through the B.S.:** This book gives you the no-nonsense rules and tips to start playing without looking like a total idiot.
- **Laugh Your Bum Off:** It's fun and keeps you entertained, even if your pickleball skills are stuck in first gear. Expect humor, sass, and the occasional profanity thrown in for good measure.
- **Master the Basics (or at Least Pretend):** We're not here to turn you into a pro; we're here to make sure you can at least hold your own without embarrassing yourself. Learn how to serve, score, and avoid the dreaded kitchen with style and maybe even a bit of swagger.
- **Understand the *Bleep*-ing Pickleball Rules:** No more awkwardly asking, "What the heck is a dink?" or pretending you didn't just step into the kitchen. This book has your back.
- **Relatable AF:** Whether you're a newbie or a seasoned player, you'll find yourself nodding along,

laughing, and maybe even shouting, "That's so me!"
- **Perfect for Gifting (or Guilt-Tripping)**: Know someone who thinks they're a pickleball god but can't serve to save their life? This book is the perfect passive-aggressive gift to help them out. Plus, this book makes the ideal bribe-uh, we mean, gift for that friend who needs a gentle (or not-so-gentle) push to join you onto the court.

Welcome to the wonderful world of pickleball. It's weird. It's fun. It's just a read away from becoming your new obsession.

Now, let's do this!

JUST ONE MORE GAME?

CHAPTER 1: WHAT THE HECK IS PICKLEBALL?

PICKLE WHAT NOW!?

Pickleball is like the beautiful, chaotic love child of tennis, badminton, and ping-pong. It's played on a baby-sized court with a paddle that looks like it was ripped from a giant's ping-pong set and a plastic ball with holes (apparently, someone thought tennis was too hard). Whether you're a seasoned athlete or just someone looking to burn off that extra slice of pizza, pickleball is the sport for you.

Whether you're a finely-tuned athlete or someone who only moves fast when there's chocolate involved, pickleball is the sport you never knew you needed. It's easy, it's addictive, and it's your new obsession. So, get ready to ditch whatever boring exercise routine you were pretending to enjoy because pickleball is here to make you sweat and laugh, sometimes at the same time.

Why You'll Be Obsessed With It

Anyone Can Play (We Didn't Say Well, But You Can Have A Blast)

You don't need to be an Olympic athlete to pick up pickleball. Most people can learn the basics faster than they can order a latte.

Look, no one has time to learn complicated rules or develop skills that take years to master. Lucky for you, pickleball is as easy as it gets. If you can hold a paddle and smack a ball, you're already halfway to being a pickleball pro, or at least good enough to fool your friends. The rules? Simple. The court? Manageable. The learning curve? Barely. You'll play like a champ faster than you can say, "Pickle what?" Forget Olympic-level training; all you need is a willingness to laugh at yourself and a paddle that doesn't look too ridiculous.

Fun for All Ages

Whether you're playing with kids, friends, or even the family members you're trying to avoid, everyone can enjoy the game together.

Pickleball is the great unifier of the sports world. It doesn't matter if you're a kid, a grandparent, or that annoying cousin who thinks they're good at everything; pickleball welcomes you all. It's the perfect game for family gatherings where you need a break from small talk or when you want to crush your loved ones in a friendly (or not-so-friendly) competition. Whether you're dodging questions about your life choices from your mother-in-law or just trying to keep the peace, pickleball's got your back. And who knows? You might even start to enjoy spending time with your family.

Burn Calories While You Laugh

Pickleball is sneaky. While you're busy having fun, it's secretly getting you in shape. It's like getting fit without even trying.

Here's the best part: while you're busy laughing at your own terrible shots, you're actually getting in shape. That's right, pickleball is a workout in disguise. You'll be running around like a maniac, swinging that paddle like you actually know what you're doing, and before you know it, you'll have burned off last night's margaritas. And let's be real: laughing at yourself is probably the best ab workout there is. So, go ahead and indulge in that extra slice of pizza. Pickleball's got your back and your waistline.

A Game for Everyone (Even You, Yes You)

Pickleball isn't just a game; it's a cult—er, I mean, community. Once you're in, you're hooked. Friendships will be made, rivalries will be born, and you'll wonder why you ever wasted your time with other sports. So, grab a paddle and get ready to become one of us.

Pickleball isn't just a game. It's a bizarre, wonderful community of people who are just as obsessed with this sport as you're about to be. You'll make friends, enemies, and maybe even frenemies, all while chasing a plastic ball around a tiny court. Whether you're here to dominate or just to have a good time, pickleball welcomes you with open arms and a slightly judgmental eye.

So, what are you waiting for? Get out there, grab that paddle, and prepare to become a pickleball addict. If you are like the rest of the world, once you start, there's no going back, just a whole lot of fun, competition, and the occasional sore loser. In the world of pickleball, the rules are simple, the laughs are plenty, and the kitchen is always off-limits.

What You Need To Play Pickleball

Who are we kidding? All you really need is a paddle, a ball, and a place to play. Sure, you'll probably end up buying every piece of pickleball swag you can find and strutting onto the court like a walking advertisement, but for now, let's keep it simple. Don't worry; we've all shown up looking like we raided the entire pickleball aisle at least once. Fake it till you make it, and soon enough, you'll be serving in style (or at least looking the part). Bare minimum gear is all you need to get started. And hey, don't forget your sense of humor. It's the most essential piece of equipment you'll ever own!

Paddle

Think of your paddle as your weapon of choice in this battle of plastic balls and bruised egos. It's big enough to make you feel powerful but light enough that you won't sprain anything important. You want something big enough to give you that satisfying "smack" when you hit the ball but light enough that you won't end up nursing a wrist injury after your first match. And let's be honest, half the fun of playing pickleball is looking good while doing it. So, pick a paddle that screams, "I may not know what I'm doing, but I'm going to look damn good doing it."

Bonus: Pick one that looks cool; looking good is half the

battle.

Pickleball

This little perforated wonder might look like it belongs in your childhood backyard, but don't let its wiffle ball vibes fool you. It's got a surprising ability to make you question your life choices, laugh out loud, and feel victorious, all in one game. The wiffle ball vibes are real, but this little guy is the heart of the game, ready to serve up equal parts joy and frustration. Get ready to chase it down like your pride depends on it.

Court (Finding Your Pickleball Playground)

So, you're ready to play but don't know where to start? Fear not! The beauty of pickleball is that it can be played just about anywhere. Local public parks are a goldmine for courts. Just look for the ones with groups of people having way more fun than the tennis players next door. If you're feeling a bit posh, check out private clubs that cater to the pickleball crowd (yes, they exist), or swing by your community center, where they've probably converted every spare inch into a makeshift pickleball court. Town recreational leagues are another great option if you're looking to make new friends or frenemies while you play. And for the DIY enthusiast, your driveway can easily transform into a pickleball paradise with a bit of tape and an at-home net. Bottom line? There's always a place to play. You just have to find it. Now, get out there and claim your court.

Optional Gear (But Who Are We Kidding? You Want This)

Shoes

Wear something that won't trip you up or make you regret that third margarita. You're going to be doing a lot of quick movements, so leave the flip-flops at home. Find a pair of shoes with a good grip and enough support to keep you upright, even when you're lunging for that impossible shot. Nobody wants to be the person who faceplants during a game because they thought their beach sandals were good enough.

Water Bottle

You're going to sweat, even if it's just from laughing. Whether you're sweating from the exertion or from the sheer embarrassment of that last missed shot, you'll want to stay hydrated. A cool water bottle is the perfect accessory to your new athletic persona.

Pro tip: Take a sip after every point. It's the ultimate time-killer when you need a break from getting your butt handed to you.

Ready, Set, Suck Less

The best part about pickleball? You don't need much to get started. In fact, that's part of its charm. With just a paddle, a ball, and a spot to play, you're in! There's no need for fancy gear or expensive memberships; just bring your enthusiasm and a sense of humor, and you're golden. So, grab your gear, hit the court, and get ready to discover how something so simple can make you so hilariously obsessed - and competitive.

What Your Pickleball Paddle Says About You

Your pickleball paddle isn't just a hunk of material; it's basically an extension of your personality, like a horoscope you can swing. It's a reflection of your innermost desires, a mirror to your soul (okay, maybe not *that* deep, but close enough). Here's what your paddle is really saying about you:

The Classic Wooden Paddle: "I'm old school. I don't need fancy gear to wipe the floor with you. I kick butt with the same paddle I've had since the dawn of time."

The Super High-Tech Carbon Fiber Paddle: "I'm serious about this. Like, really serious. I probably have a spreadsheet tracking every game I've ever played. Data is life."

The Budget Paddle from the Big Box Store: "I may have bought this on a whim, but don't underestimate me. I'm just here for the fun, but I'll still take you down with pure enthusiasm."

The Custom-Designed Paddle: "Look at me! I'm all about style and standing out. And yes, my paddle does match my outfit. If you're going to play, you might as well look good doing it."

CHAPTER 2: THE BASICS OF PLAYING

HOW TO PRETEND YOU KNOW WHAT YOU ARE DOING

Alright, so you've decided to show up with a paddle in one hand and possibly a coffee in the other. Congratulations! You've already won the first battle, getting off the couch. Seriously, just by showing up, you're ahead of half the population, so give yourself a gold star. The trick is to keep that momentum going by pretending you know what you're doing on the court. Confidence is your new best friend. Walk onto that court like you own the place, even if the last time you held a paddle was in elementary school in P.E. class. Just remember: if you look like you know what you're doing, half the battle is already won (the other half is not falling on your face).

Serving

Let's start with the serve, which is basically your way of saying, "I got this." Forget fancy tennis overhand serves. This isn't a "pinkies up" tennis match hosted on the fine grasses of London. You're going to serve underhand like you're tossing a beach ball to a toddler. Aim for the opposite box; if it lands anywhere in the vicinity, take a moment to bask in your own glory. If it lands in, congrats, you've already exceeded expectations. Now, don't trip on your way back to your spot; that's a key part of the strategy.

Rallying

Now that your serve didn't completely suck, it's time to rally. Rallying is where you smack the ball back and forth like you actually know what "rallying" means. The goal here is simple: hit the ball where your opponent isn't or where they can't reach it without doing something ridiculous. If you make them run like a caffeinated squirrel, even better. Should they miss entirely, act like it was all part of your carefully crafted plan. Remember, style points matter, so keep that "I meant to do that" look on your face.

Scoring Points

Points are the currency of pickleball, and let's be honest, they're even better than real money since they come with bragging rights. You score when your opponent screws up, whether they launch the ball into orbit, smash it into the net, or do something truly embarrassing (bonus points for that last one). Just remember: only the serving team can score. So, if you're not serving, clap politely, pretend you're strategizing for your next turn, and try not to look too eager.

Tips For Pretending You're A Pro

Aim for Consistency

Power is nice, but forget trying to be the pickleball version of a legendary goddess-like set of tennis sisters. What you really want is consistency. Get that ball over the net and keep it in bounds. If you keep launching the ball into the parking lot, you might want to dial it back. Trust us, being the player who doesn't screw up is way more valuable than being the person who smashes every shot out of the park.

Stay Ready

Pickleball is unpredictable, like a preschool class on a sugar high. Always be prepared to move because pickleball is fast-paced. Stay on your toes, and don't be afraid to dive for the ball like it's the last piece of chocolate. Sure, you might look like a flailing muppet, but you're a flailing muppet who's in the game. Just keep moving and try not to look like your shoes are cemented to the court.

The Golden Rule

Pickleball is meant to be fun — be kind! If you're not having fun, or you're being a playground meanie, you're doing it wrong. The more you play with different levels and types of players, the better you'll get (hopefully) and the more fun you'll have, so get out there and make some memories (and maybe you'll match up with your next best friend).

Pickleball Rules For Dumm-, I Mean, Anyone

Let's break this down so that even a dumm—, uh, anyone can understand. This book is your quick and dirty guide to stepping onto the pickleball court like you've been playing games and taking names for years. Think of this as the cheat sheet you wish you had for those school projects you totally procrastinated on, only this time, it's actually fun and way less stressful.

The Essential Pickleball Rules

Serving Rules

Stand behind the baseline, pretend you know what you're doing, and serve the ball underhand for crying out loud (you'd be surprised how many get this wrong— read the room, people). Aim for the opposite service box, and pray it lands in bounds. If it does, congratulations, you're already better than half of us.

The ball has to bounce once on each side before the real fun begins. In other words, the third shot. Then, you can run into the court crossing the baseline (but stay out of the kitchen). This prevents your overzealous friends from smashing it into oblivion right off the bat.

Rules of Rallying

Once the serve is in play, the ball can either bounce or be smacked right out of the air. The idea is to hit it where your opponent isn't or make them chase that little plastic ball of delight to reach it.

Scoring Points

First to 11 points wins, but (of course) you've got to win by 2. Only the serving team can score, so if you're not serving, well, tough luck.

Points are yours when your opponent screws up, like hitting it out of bounds or into the net. Sit back and enjoy their misery as you rack up the points. Don't forget to be a good sport, play fair, and pretend to care about their delicate egos.

Fault Rules

Hit the ball out of bounds? That's a fault. Serve it into the net? Fault. Step into the kitchen while trying to look fabulous? Fault and everyone's yelling, "Stay out of the kitchen!"

Keep It Simple, Stupid (K.I.S.S.)

Pickleball is supposed to be fun, so don't overthink it. Follow these rules, laugh at your mistakes, and remember: the goal today is to have a good time, not to become the next touring pickleball pro (yet).

Consistency Over Power

Before you try to obliterate the ball like you're in an action movie, just aim to get it over the net and in play. That's where the real skill lies. Just focus on getting it over the net and keeping it in bounds. Trust me, that's already half the battle.

With these basics in your back pocket, you'll hit the court with the confidence of a seasoned pro or someone who can convincingly fake it.

The Kitchen Rule (Not For Cooking!)

What the Heck Is the Kitchen Anyway?

Welcome to the kitchen, no, not the one where you burn toast. In pickleball, the kitchen is the no-smash zone that keeps things civilized. The Kitchen Rule separates the pros from the 'I-have-no-idea-what-I'm-doing' crowd. So, let's break it down and learn why this is the one kitchen you'll actually want to avoid.

The "No Fun Allowed" Zone

The kitchen is the area closest to the net, also known as the non-volley zone (or the one rectangle where fun comes with restrictions). It's where your dreams of smashing the ball from up close go to die.

It's 7 feet of "don't even think about it," marked by a line that you better respect if you want to avoid the scorn of your fellow players.

"Stay Out of the Kitchen" Rule

You can't step into the kitchen to volley the ball (hit it out of the air). The ball must bounce first before you can step in and do your thing.

This rule exists to keep things fair and prevent anyone from getting too aggressive at the net. It also gives everyone an excuse to shout, "Stay out of the kitchen!", which, let's be honest, is pretty fun.

Why It's Important

The kitchen rule adds a layer of strategy to the game. You have to be mindful of your positioning and avoid stepping into the kitchen unless the ball has bounced.

Otherwise, you'll get called out faster than you can say "pickleball."

How To Avoid Looking Like An Idiot In The Kitchen

Stay Behind the Line

When you're playing at the net, hang out just behind the kitchen line. You will prepare yourself with self-talk and be ready to volley without stepping into the forbidden zone and getting a penalty.

Anticipate the Bounce

Watch for opportunities to move into the kitchen after the ball bounces. Take advantage of this chance to show off, just don't trip over the line in your excitement.

Master the Kitchen (Don't Burn Down the House)

The kitchen is where games are often won or lost, so learn how to navigate it without stepping on any toes (literally). Respect the line, know when to stay out, and soon you'll be ruling the court like a pro.

How To Serve Like A Champ

Mastering the Art of Not Screwing Up the Serve

Ah, the serve, the moment where you either shine like a pickleball god or completely botch it and hope no one notices. Mastering the art of not screwing up the serve is like learning to pour a cup of coffee without spilling: deceptively simple but oh so satisfying when you nail it. You got this and can start the point on the right foot, so let's dive in and make sure your serve doesn't become the stuff of your opponent's highlight reel.

Start Strong (Serve Like a Fast Food Chain at Lunchtime)

Stand behind the baseline, feet shoulder-width apart, and channel your inner zen. Hold the paddle like you know what you're doing (even if you don't), and prepare to serve.

Swing underhand like you're throwing a slow pitch at a county fair. Your paddle should stay below your waist when you hit the ball; no fancy stuff here.

The Swing

Aim diagonally across the court, and if the ball lands in the service box, you're golden. If not, well, better luck next time.

Remember: Follow through with your swing. Not only does it look cool, but it also helps keep your serve under control. Plus, you can pretend it was intentional if things go south.

Follow Through

After you've served, try not to stand there looking shocked that it worked. Be ready to move and keep the rally going.

Keep your eye on the ball. Now is your chance to get

the upper hand, so don't blow it by daydreaming about what you'll have for lunch.

Pro Tips (Seriously, Do Yourself A Favor)

Practice Your Aim

If you can get the ball to land where you want it to, you're already ahead of most players. Mix up your serves to keep your opponents guessing. No one likes a predictable player.

Stay Calm

A calm, controlled serve is often more effective than a wild, powerful one. So take a deep breath, focus on placement, and try not to overthink it (even though you definitely will).

Serve to Win (You Deserve to Dream Big)

Your serve sets the tone for the point, so don't mess it up. With a bit of practice (and maybe some divine intervention), you'll be serving like a champ, or at a minimum, someone who knows which end of the paddle to hold.

How To Perfect Your Shots (So You Can Finally Win A Point)

You go! You've mastered the art of not embarrassing yourself on the serve! It's time to step up your game and win a point. Perfecting your shots is where you go from "just happy to be here" to "actually knows what they're doing." Whether you're aiming for a killer forehand, a sneaky dink, or a smash that makes your opponents question their life choices, this section will guide you through turning your wild swings into point-scoring magic. Let's make sure your shots aren't just impressive; they're downright unstoppable.

Forehand and Backhand

Your forehand is your bread and butter; it's where your power comes from. But don't neglect your backhand unless you want to be the person everyone targets (and laughs at).

Keep your paddle face square to the ball and aim for smooth, controlled swings. The more fluid your motion, the less likely you are to hit the ball into the next zip code.

The Dink (No, It's Not an Insult)

A dink is a soft, gentle shot that just barely clears the net and lands close to it while within a 7-foot barrier known as the infamous kitchen. It's like a tap on the shoulder that says, "Gotcha!" Use it to frustrate your opponents and make them question their life choices.

Dinks are strategic; they slow down the game and force your opponents to come to the net, where they'll likely screw up.

The Volley

A volley is when you hit the ball out of the air before it

bounces. It's aggressive, fast, and exactly what you need to keep your opponents on their toes (or make them trip over their own feet).

Practice quick, sharp volleys to increase your chances of winning points at the net. Just don't get too cocky. Volleying is harder than it looks.

Winning Strategies (Better Than Not-Losing Strategies)

Placement over Power

You don't need to hit the ball like you're trying to send it to Mars. Focus on placing it where your opponents aren't. It's sneaky and effective and way more satisfying when it works.

Control the Pace

Mix up your shots with a combination of dinks, volleys, and deep shots. Keep your opponents guessing, and you'll keep them on the defensive.

Play Smart (Even If You're Faking It)

Remember, pickleball is as much about strategy as it is about skill. Use your brain (yes, you have one) to outplay your opponents, and you'll find yourself winning more often or at least looking like you know what you're doing.

CHAPTER 3: PICKLEBALL SCORING MADNESS

CALLING THE SCORE: WAIT, WHAT'S MY NUMBER AGAIN?

Whether you're new to the game or a seasoned player who still can't figure out why you're yelling "1-4-2" at your partner, we will walk you through the basics, along with a few laughs. Ready? Let's score some points!

Before every serve, the serving team must announce the score, which has three parts:

1. **Your Score** (the server's score).
2. **Your Opponent's Score** (the people you're trying to humiliate—uh, beat).
3. **Server Number** (1 or 2, depending on who's serving).

Let's walk through it together; if your team has 3 points, and your opponents have 4, you'd say "3-4-1" if you're the first server. Confused? Don't worry, you're in good company. Just remember: your score first, their score second, and whether you're Server 1 or 2 third. And here's a pro tip: if you can't remember whether you're Server 1 or 2, just throw a desperate look at your partner. They'll either help you or give you a good ol' eye roll. Either way, problem solved.

Serving First? There's One More Caveat to Keep You on Your Toes

You're the first server of the game. Lucky you! Well, kind

of. The first serve of a game is a bit tricky. You'll kick things off by calling out "0-0-2." Yes, you read that right, *two*. But don't worry, it's not a typo or some secret code. The reason for that "2" is simple: during the very first serve of the game, only one person on your team gets to serve. It's the universe's way of making sure that the advantage of serving first isn't too overwhelming. Fair, right? After this initial serve, things return to normal, and both partners get to serve before handing it over to the other team.

So, to sum it up, kick things off with "0-0-2," after that, keep your scores straight, switch sides when you're supposed to, and try not to overthink it. Easy, right? Now go serve like you mean it!

Switching Servers: When It All Goes Wrong (It Will)

Alright, here's where things get a little tangled, like trying to untangle Christmas lights you swore you wrapped neatly last year. In pickleball, when you or your partner loses a point while serving, the baton (or paddle, in this case) passes to the other player on your team. So if you're Player 1 and you screw up, congratulations! Your partner now gets to take over as Server 2. But if both of you manage to fumble the serve (don't worry, it happens more often than anyone wants to admit), the serve gets yanked out of your hands entirely and handed over to the other team. This momentous occasion is known as a "side out," usually accompanied by groans, sighs, and the temptation to throw your paddle dramatically to the ground (resist the urge).

Confused About Who's Serving? You're Not Alone

If you lose track of who's supposed to serve next (and trust us, it happens to the best of us), just switch it up until someone on the other side of the net complains. Honestly, nobody really knows what's going on half the time anyway, and you might just get away with it.

Side Outs: The Great Reset (Snack Break?)

So, you've reached that dreaded side-out moment? Don't sweat it. Milk it as a chance to catch your breath, grab a drink, or pretend to stretch while you mentally prepare for the next round of chaos. Here's the deal: after both you and your partner fail to win a point while serving, the serve switches to the other team, and the serving team gets to swap sides of the court. (No, you can't just stay on your favorite side no matter how much you love that shady corner). The receiving team? They stay put, silently judging your every move.

A Simple Summary (Cause You've Got Better Things To Do)

Okay, here is a quick and dirty summary. You're welcome. We know reading can be painstaking when you could be playing pickleball instead!

When your team begins to serve, start on the right side of the court. If you win that point, you get to keep serving, but now you switch to the left side. Think of it as a mini cha-cha-cha: right, left, right, left, just with less rhythm and more sweat. If you lose a point, no biggie; your partner takes over and does the same little dance. But if both of you manage to lose (don't worry, it's basically a rite of passage), the other team gets to serve. That's called a "side out," which is fancy for, "Let's give the other team a turn before we embarrass ourselves further."

And hey, when you're receiving front the serving side? Just stay put. Only the serving team gets the fun of switching sides.

The TL;DR?

Serve from the right, switch sides when you win, let your partner take over when you lose and try not to walk into each other.

CHAPTER 4: PICKLEBALL ETIQUETTE (HOW TO NOT BE 'THAT PLAYER')

Don't Be 'That Player' on the Court

P ickleball is a game of sportsmanship and respect. Shake hands (or tap paddles) after the game, and always be polite to your opponents. Yes, even the ones who annoy the heck out of you.

Call the score loudly and clearly before serving. Jumping on the chance to yell something out isn't just for show. It's so everyone knows what the heck is going on. Don't be the person who "forgets" to call the score when you're losing.

Wait Your Turn

If you need to walk across another court, wait until the point is over. It's a small courtesy that keeps everyone safe and focused, and it means you won't get hit by a stray ball.

If you're waiting to play, don't hover like a vulture. Give the players on the court some space and maybe some privacy while you're at it.

Call Your Own Lines (And Don't Be a Tool About It)

In pickleball, players are responsible for calling the lines on their side of the court. Be fair and honest. If the ball is close, give your opponent the benefit of the doubt. Karma will reward you later (maybe).

And remember, if you're constantly calling balls out that are obviously in, everyone will start to hate you.

And nobody wants that.

Keep the Game Fun

Pickleball is supposed to be enjoyable. Unless you are a professional, don't get too serious. It's all about having a good time with friends and family. If you're not having fun, you're doing it wrong.

Be Nice. It's Not That Hard. Seriously.

Stay Positive (Even When You're Losing)

Win or lose, keep a positive attitude. Congratulate your opponents on good shots, and don't dwell on mistakes. No one likes a sore loser or a gloating winner.

Be Patient (Seriously, Calm the *Bleep* Down)

If you're playing with beginners, be patient and encouraging. Everyone starts somewhere, and your support will help them enjoy the game and maybe even want to play with you again.

Golden Rule Of Pickleball: Don't Be A Tool (Even If You're A 5.0 Hotshot)

Listen, we get it. You're the 5.0 pickleball wizard who smashes shots faster than a newbie can say, "What's a dink?" But here's the thing: just because you're a quantified expert doesn't mean you get to squash the newbies like bugs on the court. The Golden Rule of

Pickleball is simple: treat others how you'd want to be treated, even if they're still figuring out which end of the paddle to hold.

So, instead of serving up a humiliation sandwich, add a little respect, kindness, and humor to your game. Be the player everyone actually *wants* to play with, not the one who makes them consider taking up chess instead. Remember, you were a newbie once, too (yes, even you). So, smile, laugh, and try not to make your superiority too obvious. Who knows? You might even make a friend instead of just another opponent.

CHAPTER5: PICKLEBALL ALTER EGO (DON'T BE THAT PERSON)

UNMASKING THE PICKLEBALL CHARACTERS (YES, THAT ANNOYING

PLAYER MIGHT BE YOU)

L et's face it: when you step onto that pickleball court, something changes. You're not just [Your Name] anymore; you're channeling a whole new alter ego. Whether you're the calm strategist who's secretly plotting everyone's demise or the wild smasher who thinks every shot is a chance to destroy, we all have a pickleball persona lurking within us. So, who are you really when the paddle is in your hand? Time to embrace your inner court creature and find out which pickleball alter ego is running the show. Spoiler: We're all a little bit insane out there.

The Gearhead

Oh, look, it's Captain Gearhead! You know, the type who shows up to the court decked out like they're sponsored by a pickleball brand you've never heard of. New paddle? Check. Shoes that cost more than your rent? Double-check. They've got all the gear and are here to remind you of it. What they lack in actual skill, they make up for in flashy outfits and a paddle that's more high-tech than your smartphone. But hey, if looking like a pro was the same as playing like one, they'd be on the cover of a magazine. Instead, they're just trying to figure out why all that gear hasn't magically made them any better. But they sure look cool, don't they?

The Socialite

Pickleball? Oh, you mean Social Hour on the court. For the Socialite, the game is just an excuse to chat, mingle, and organize the post-game margaritas. They're less concerned with winning and more focused on who's bringing snacks to the next match. You'll see them high-fiving everyone, even when they miss a shot. Who cares? It's all about the vibes, man. If a group of people is laughing loudly and not paying attention to the game, you can bet the Socialite is at the center of it. And honestly, who doesn't love someone who makes losing feel like a party?

The Ratings Bragger

Ah, the Ratings Bragger. What's the point of playing if you can't remind everyone they have the largest DUPR score every five minutes? This player has their rating tattooed on their brain, and they're ready to drop it into conversation at the slightest provocation. Just score a point? "That's why I'm a 4.0, baby!" Missed a shot? "Guess that's why I'm not a 4.5 yet." They're so obsessed with their rating, they probably dream in decimals. And yes, they'll tell you all about their latest win streak, whether you ask or not. Just smile, nod, and try not to inflate their oversized ego.

The Tech Bro

Welcome to Silicon Valley on the pickleball court. The Tech Bro is here with all the gadgets, smartwatches, apps, and probably a drone to capture their "epic" serves. They've got data on everything: swing speed, heart rate, the temperature of their sweat. If it's tech-related, they've got it, and they'll let you know that your "old-school" approach is cute but outdated. Strategy? Nah, they've got an algorithm for that. It's like they're trying to win a startup pitch instead of a pickleball game. Just don't be surprised if they ask you to invest in their new pickleball tracking app by the end of the match.

The Banger

Subtlety? Never heard of it. The Banger is here to smash every shot like it owes them money. Dinking? That's for people who like to play "soft." The Banger has one goal: hitting the ball as hard as humanly possible and watching it soar. If you're looking for finesse, look somewhere else because this player is all about power, baby. They'll drive every ball straight at you with enough force to make you question your life choices. And when the ball flies out of bounds? That just means it wasn't fast enough to stay on the court. Watch out; when the Banger steps up, it's smash or be smashed.

The Question Asker

You know that friend who can't stop asking questions? That's the Question Asker on the pickleball court. What's the rule again? Can you really do that? Wait, what's a dink? They're full of questions and are not afraid to ask them mid-game. Every point is an opportunity to learn something new, whether the rest of us want to or not. But hey, knowledge is power, right?

Even if it does slow the game down to a crawl. Just be ready with answers, or you'll be there all day while they figure out what the heck's going on.

The Strategist

You think you're playing pickleball, but the Strategist is playing 4D chess. Every move is calculated, and every shot is part of a master plan. While you're just trying to get the ball over the net, they're thinking three steps ahead, setting traps like a goddamn action film villain. You might win a point, but don't get too comfortable; they've already figured out how to make you regret it. Good luck if you're up against a Strategist. You're gonna need it. Just don't be surprised if you find yourself completely outmaneuvered and wondering how the bleep they did that.

The Natural Athlete

Oh, great, the Natural Athlete is here. You know, the one who's good at every sport they try, including pickleball. They've been playing for all of five minutes, and they're already dominating the court like it's no big deal. While you're struggling to keep up, they're smashing winners and casually asking if you want to "go again." It's almost unfair, but then again, life isn't fair, is it? Just try not to be too bitter when they make it look so damn easy. After all, they're just here to have fun - even if it means crushing your spirit in the process.

The Pickleball Purist

Meet the Pickleball Purist, the guardian of all things

pickleball. They know the rulebook by heart and will not hesitate to call you out for the tiniest infraction. Kitchen foot fault? They're on it. Improper serve? Don't even try it. The Purist believes in playing the game the "right" way, and they'll make sure everyone else does too. It's like having a referee on the court, only they're playing too. If you're in a game with a Purist, be ready to follow the rules to the letter, they definitely are. And if you think you can bend the rules a little? Think again, buddy.

The Reluctant Player

You can spot the Reluctant Player from a mile away. They're the ones who got dragged onto the court by their overly enthusiastic friend or loved one and still aren't sure what they're doing here. They're playing, sure, but they're not exactly thrilled about it. Maybe they'll start to enjoy it, maybe not. But for now, they're just trying to survive the game without embarrassing themselves. Hey, at least they showed up, right? If you're lucky, they may be your first victim, and you will have a chance to actually win one. But don't count on them sticking around for the next game unless there's free beer.

The Pickleball Lobster

Ah, the Pickleball Lobster, the player who lives to lob the ball so high, you'll need a telescope to see it. They don't care about fancy shots or quick points; they're here to make you run. And run you will, back and forth, chasing down those sky-high lobs until your legs give out. It's not pretty, but it's effective. While you're huffing and puffing, the Lobster is cool as a cucumber, ready to send another ball into the stratosphere. Hate it all you want, but you've gotta admit, it works. Just try not to curse too loudly when you're sprinting for the umpteenth time.

Pickle Bros

These guys roll up to the court like it's a gym, shirts optional, muscles mandatory. They've got the priciest gear money can buy. Clearly, performance is all about the size of the paddle, right? But when it comes to actual gameplay, let's just say their technique is as basic as their protein shakes. They may not win many games, but they'll definitely win the award for most flexed biceps and loudest grunts. For the Pickle Bros, it's not about how you play but how you look while doing it.

CHAPTER 6: QUICK FIXES FOR YOUR PICKLEBALL MISHAPS

How to Suck Less (Minimal Effort)

We all have those moments on the court where things just go south fast. But fear not! You don't need to morph into a pro overnight to stop looking like you've never held a paddle before. Here's your survival guide to quick fixes for those oh-so-common pickleball mistakes. Sometimes, sucking a little less is all it takes to turn the game around.

Missing Your Serve? (Welcome to the Club)

What's Happening: You may be hitting the ball too hard, or your aim is more questionable than your life choices.

Quick Fix: Slow down, take a breath, and focus on making a controlled, accurate serve. Aim for the middle of the service box. Hitting it out of bounds is just embarrassing.

Hitting the Ball Out of Bounds (Again)

What's Happening: You're putting way too much power behind your shots, trying to look like a badass.

Quick Fix: Dial it back and focus on control. Try hitting the ball with a bit more finesse and less "let's see if I can break a window."

Getting Stuck in the Kitchen (And Not in a Good Way)

What's Happening: You're stepping into the kitchen to volley, which is against the rules (and yes, everyone saw you do it).

Quick Fix: Practice staying just behind the kitchen line when you're at the net. Practicing this will help you get used to avoiding stepping in and committing a fault.

Not Moving Your Feet (Don't be Lazy... Let's Go!)

What's Happening: You're getting caught flat-footed, making it hard to reach the ball and even harder to maintain your dignity.

Quick Fix: Stay on the balls of your feet and be ready to move quickly. Good footwork is key to getting to the ball on time and not looking like a total boob.

Practice Makes You Slightly Less Terrible

Let's face it. You didn't pick up that paddle to just "have fun." You want to win, and not just once in a while, but so often that your friends start rethinking why they are even friends with you. Well, to become the pickleball legend you're destined to be, you've got to practice like you mean it. And no, that doesn't mean just showing up and hoping for the best.

Master the Third Shot Drop

Think of the third shot drop as your secret weapon. You know, like when you tell everyone you're just here for a good time, and then BAM, you pull out a killer move they never saw coming. Try to land the third shot of the point in the kitchen so you don't set up your opponents to smash the ball in your face. Nail this shot, and you'll have your opponents tripping over their own feet, wondering how you became a pickleball god overnight.

Refine Your Dinking Strategy (No, Not a Typo for Drinking)

No, dinking isn't just a typo in the book for the word drinking. Dinking is a soft tapping of the ball and hoping for the best. It's an art form. Think of it like the perfect slow clap in a movie: you want to build tension, draw them in, and then, they fall right into your trap. A good dink game is like psychological warfare with a paddle. Keep them guessing; they'll be too busy overthinking to notice you've already won the point.

Improve Your Court Positioning

You and your partner must move together like you're in a synchronized swimming routine, without the nose plugs and weird bathing caps. Stay in sync, and you'll be covering the court like a pro. Bonus points if you manage to do it without shouting, "Yours!" every five seconds.

Master the Lob and Counter-Lob

The lob is your way of saying, "Hey, remember all those smash shots you love so much? Yeah, good luck with that." Perfect this move, and watch as your opponents scramble to the back of the court like they're late for a flight. When they lob it back, they get ready to rain down some justice with an overhead smash that makes them regret ever stepping on the court.

Develop a Killer Serve and Return

Your serve is the first impression of the match, so make it count. Add some spin, some speed, maybe a little flair, and watch your opponent's confidence crumble. And when you're returning, aim to send a message: "Nice try, but you're going to have to do better than that." Basically, make them question why they even bothered showing up today.

Stay Positive (Hold Your Tantrum for the Ride Home)

Everyone makes mistakes, especially when learning something new. The important thing is to learn from them and keep enjoying the game. Remember, you're not in this alone. Everyone else is screwing up too. So, laugh it off and keep playing.

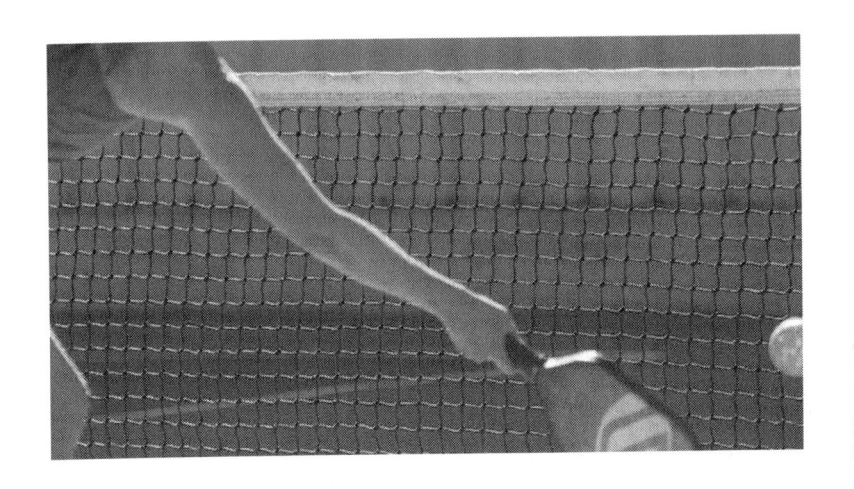

CHAPTER 7: HOW TO PRACTICE ON YOUR OWN

How to Get Better Without an Audience

So, you want to get better at pickleball without the pressure of an audience? Smart move. Practicing solo means you can work on your skills without anyone watching you whiff that serve, or worse, hearing their unsolicited advice. In this chapter, we'll show you how to up your game all by yourself. From wall drills to shadow swings, you'll be a pickleball ninja in no time. And hey, when you finally hit the court with friends, they'll wonder when you got so darn good.

Serve Practice

Set up targets in the service box and practice aiming for them. Try to be consistent in placing your serves in different spots so that you can be the master of deception on the court. Plus, hitting a target feels way more satisfying than missing it completely.

Wall Drills (Don't Worry, Walls Don't Judge)

Find a wall and hit the ball against it repeatedly. Wall Drills will help you improve your reaction time, hand-eye coordination, and control. It's also a great way to practice volleys without anyone watching you mess up.

Footwork Drills (Try Not to Trip over Your Own Feet)

Practice moving side-to-side and forward and backward on the court without a ball. Focus on staying light on your feet and being ready to move in any direction quickly. Imagine you're dodging imaginary pickleballs, or maybe just your own inner demons.

Shadow Swinging (It's Not as Weird as It Sounds)

Practice your forehand and backhand swings without the ball. Regular practice helps reinforce muscle memory and perfect your form. Bonus: You get to look like you're fighting invisible ninjas.

Target Practice

Place cones or targets on the court and aim to hit them with your shots. Target Practice will help you work on accuracy and placement. Plus, you can pretend the targets are the faces of your enemies.

Keep It Fun (No One Likes a Yawn Fest)

Solo practice doesn't have to be boring. Set challenges for yourself, like hitting certain targets in a row or making several consecutive volleys. The more fun you make it, the more you'll improve. And if all else fails, bribe yourself with snacks.

CHAPTER 8: RECRUIT, BRIBE, OR BLACKMAIL: GETTING YOUR PEOPLE TO PLAY

How to Get Everyone to Play

(Without Resorting to Begging)

So you've caught the pickleball bug and are now itching to drag everyone you know into the madness. But how do you get your friends, family, or that stubborn neighbor to pick up a paddle without looking desperate? Don't worry; we've got your back. In this chapter, we'll explore the art of persuasion, whether it's gentle coaxing, outright bribery, or, if all else fails, a little bit of blackmail. Let's be honest: pickleball is more fun when you've got a crew. And by the end of this, they'll be as hooked as you are (even if they don't know it yet).

Start with the Fun Factor (That's What It's All about)

Highlight how easy and fun pickleball is to learn. Emphasize that it's a game everyone can enjoy, regardless of age or athletic ability. The social, relaxed atmosphere makes it perfect for casual play or for convincing your friends and family that this is the best idea you've ever had.

Plus, it's a great way to get everyone off their couch and onto the court without them even realizing they're exercising.

Host a Pickleball Party (Parties Make Everything Better)

Invite your friends and family for a casual pickleball get-together. Set up a court, bring some snacks, and make it a fun, low-pressure introduction to the game. Consider hosting a "Pickleball and Chill" night, where everyone plays a few rounds and then relaxes with some refreshments.

And if all else fails, bribe them with food. No one can resist yummy treats.

Walk the Walk, Not Just the Talk

Show your enthusiasm for pickleball. The more excited you are about it, the more curious and eager your friends and family will be to try it. Share your experiences, funny moments, and the benefits you've noticed since you started playing.

And if they still don't join, just keep playing until they give in. Persistence pays off or annoys them into submission.

Invite Your Friends and Family (They Can't Say No Forever)

Pickleball is a fantastic way to spend time with loved ones. It's easy to learn, and it's fun for all ages. Invite your friends, family, and even neighbors to join you on the court. If they refuse, just keep asking until they give in.

Set Up a Friendly Tournament (Let the Rivalries Begin)

Organize a mini-tournament with your group. You can

mix up the teams so that everyone gets a chance to play together. Add a bit of excitement and competition to the game and a chance to crush your loved ones in a socially acceptable way.

Offer to Teach (Even If You're Not an Expert)

You've played pickleball a few times, and suddenly, you're the pro in the group. Embrace it! Offer to teach the basics to the newbies with patience and encouragement. They'll pick it up faster with your help. Run through some practice games to get them comfortable and confident. And if they're struggling, just remind them that everyone was a beginner once, even you. So go ahead and be the pickleball guru they didn't know they needed. After all, who doesn't love a know-it-all with a paddle?

Highlight the Health Benefits (Without Sounding Like a Health Nut)

Mention how pickleball is excellent for staying active and healthy without being too strenuous. It's perfect for those looking for a fun way to exercise. Share how it improves coordination, balance, and mental sharpness. Plus, it's a great way to relieve stress.

If they're still on the fence, just tell them it's better than running on a treadmill. That should do the trick.

Brag About the Social Side (Everyone Loves to Socialize)

Talk about the awesome pickleball community and how

it's a fantastic way to meet new people and make lasting friendships. Mention that pickleball is perfect for spending quality time with family, friends, or even coworkers, on and off the court.

Pickleball is the ultimate icebreaker. If that doesn't convince them, just tell them it's a great way to avoid awkward small talk at parties.

Making It a Regular Thing (So They Can't Escape)

Set up a regular pickleball night where everyone knows they're welcome to join. Whether it's once a week or once a month, make it a tradition. This way, no one can claim they "forgot" or "didn't know you were playing."

Celebrate Together (Winning Is Optional)

After the game, go out for a meal, grab some ice cream, or grab an adult beverage together. The social side of pickleball is just as important as the game itself. Plus, food always tastes better after you've worked up an appetite (even if it was just from laughing).

Building Bonds (Whether They Like It or Not)

Playing pickleball together is a great way to bond and create lasting memories. The spirit of pickleball is all about a welcoming community and connecting with people, building friendships, reconnecting with loved ones, and some are even finding love interests. Add a splash of fun gathering and competition, and let the magic happen.

Enjoy the Moments (Even If You Lose)

Whether you're playing a serious match or just having some fun, the most important thing is to enjoy the time spent with friends and family. Pickleball is the perfect excuse to get everyone together and to remind them why they love (or tolerate) you.

CHAPTER 9: WINNING WITHOUT ACTING LIKE A TOTAL FOOL (THE ART OF GOOD

SPORTSMANSHIP)

How to Crush Your Opponents Without Crushing Their Souls

Woo-hoo! Now, you've got the skills to dominate the court. Here's the straight-up tea: no one likes a sore winner (or a sore loser, for that matter). In this chapter, we're going to look at how to strut that fine line between being a fierce competitor and not being the reason people suddenly "remember" they left the stove on. We'll show you how to win without making your opponents despise you—and how to lose without sulking like you've just lost your once-in-a-lifetime spot on a hit television show where you dance around with celebrities. Because let's be real: the only thing worse than losing is winning in a way that makes everyone secretly hope you step on a small toy later. So, buckle up, and let's dive into the art of good sportsmanship—where you can crush your opponents and still leave with friends (and maybe a few frenemies).

Play Fair (Karma Has a Wicked Backhand)

Always play by the rules. No one likes the person who cheats just to win a $2 trophy or some high fives at the local court. Win with some grace, lose with even more, and for the love of all things posh, congratulate your opponents without making it sound like you're doing them a favor. Remember, the goal is to have fun—unless you're a professional pickleball player—in which case, still have fun—and if you happen to win while doing it, well, that's just the cherry on top (in the case of a pro, then there's a cash prize in the mix).

Don't Rub It in (Too Much)

Winning feels fantastic—like finding out your least favorite coworker is moving to another department—but remember to keep it friendly. Sure, you can do a little happy dance, but save the full-blown victory lap for your living room. Your goal is to have fun, not make others feel like they just lost the game *and* their dignity.

Compliment Good Play (Even If It Kills You)

Whether you're the victor or licking your wounds, always throw a compliment or two your opponents' way. It's called "sportsmanship" for a reason, and it doesn't mean you're admitting defeat—it means you're a classy player who knows how to keep it posh. Plus, who knows? They might just return the favor next time you accidentally send a ball flying into the parking lot.

Stay Lighthearted and Smile (Because Botox Is Expensive)

Even in the heat of competition, remember to keep things light. Laugh off mistakes, and don't let your face twist into something that would scare small children. It's just a game, after all, and in a week, no one's going to remember who won anyway (except you because you're going to post about it on social media).

Encourage Others (Don't Go Full Self-Help Guru)

If you see someone struggling, offer a kind word or a quick tip. Help them get better, and they'll be more likely not to "accidentally" peg you with a ball next time. But don't go overboard with the pep talk—unless you want to be known as the annoying self-help guru of the court.

How To Not Lose All Your Friends

Be a Team Player (Even If You Could've Won Alone)

In doubles, communicate with your partner. No one likes playing with someone who suddenly goes silent like they're in the middle of a reality show confessional. Work together because nothing kills the vibe faster than your partner wishing they could swap you out mid-game.

Talk It Out Before You Smash It Out (Avoid the Blame Game)

Some say the best shot in pickleball is down the middle—especially if you're married and want to test how quickly you can ruin date night. Save yourself the awkward silent treatment on the way home (or a one-way ticket to couples therapy) by figuring out who's got that middle ball. Proactive communication is key because nothing says "relationship goals," like not arguing over a missed shot in public.

Celebrate the Experience (Not Just the Victory)

At the end of the day, pickleball is about enjoying yourself, bonding with others, and maybe getting in a bit of cardio. Whether you win or lose, focus on the fun, the laughter, and the occasional trash talk that makes the game worth playing. And remember, there's always next time—so play nice, keep it posh, and don't be the reason someone "accidentally" drops a paddle on your foot.

CHAPTER 10: EXCUSES (FOR WHEN YOU'RE NOT FEELING IT)

*Creative Ways to Bow Out
(Without Losing Face)*

We've all been there: you love pickleball, but today, the thought of chasing a perforated ball around feels about as appealing as doing your taxes. Maybe you're "too tired," or perhaps your "grandma's cat needs a bath" (hey, it could happen). Whatever the excuse, this chapter is your get-out-of-jail-free card, packed with hilariously creative ways to dodge the game without looking like a total quitter. Remember, you're not avoiding the pickleball game; you're just taking a moment to win the excuse game.

The Classic "I'm Tired" Excuse:

"You know, I've been playing like a pro all day. I think it's time for a well-deserved break." It's the perfect excuse when you're feeling lazy but don't want to admit it.

The Sudden Errand Excuse:

"Oops, I just remembered I need to pick up something from the store. I better go now before I forget!" This one's great because no one can argue with it. Who's going to question your grocery needs?

The Family Call Excuse:

"I think I hear my phone ringing. It might be the kids; better check in just to be sure." Even if your phone is on silent, no one's going to argue with parental duties.

The Weather Worry Excuse:

"Looks like it might rain soon. I should probably head home before it starts pouring." Even if the sky is clear, the weather is always a plausible excuse, especially if you live somewhere unpredictable.

For You Overachievers Out There (Who Deserve A Break)

The Rest Day Excuse:

"I'm taking a rest day to let my champion muscles recover. Gotta be fresh for the next game!" It's the perfect way to bow out while still sounding like an athlete.

The Sneaky Strategy Excuse:

"I'm going to sit this one out and observe. I need to study everyone's strategies for next time." This genius makes you sound strategic, even if you're just tired of running.

Using Excuses Gracefully

Keep It Light:

When you use an excuse, do it with a smile. Keep the mood fun and light-hearted so no one feels put off. It's all in good fun, after all.

Stay Social (Even If You're Sitting Out):

Even if you're not playing, stay engaged. Cheer on your friends, offer some tips, and stay part of the action. It's the perfect way to stay involved without actually breaking a sweat.

Bow Out with Style (And Maybe a Little Dignity):

Sometimes, you just need a break, and that's okay! With the right excuse, you can take a breather while still keeping the fun going for everyone else. Plus, you can always jump back in when you're ready or when you've run out of excuses.

CHAPTER 11: PRE-GAME WARM-UP SO YOU DON'T WIPE OUT

How to Avoid Becoming a Pickleball Injury Statistic

All right, pickleball warriors, it's time to talk about safety. Nothing kills the vibe of a game faster than a trip to the ER. Sure, we all want to channel our inner pickleball pro, but let's face it, nobody wants to be remembered as the person who pulled a hammy trying to show off a killer spin shot. This chapter is your ultimate guide to staying in one piece while dominating the court. We'll cover everything from avoiding the dreaded "pickleball elbow" to making sure you don't turn a graceful dive into a viral blooper.

Because our lawyers say so, we need to take a moment to remind you that this book does not replace professional medical advice. It is intended as all in good fun—if you end up with a bruised ego or a sprained wrist, that's on you. Always check with a healthcare professional before attempting any new athletic feats or trying to serve up that winning shot.

Play smart, stay safe, and let's keep those victory laps injury-free. Limping off the court is never a good look.

Warm-Up (Not-Tearing-Your-Hamstring Plan)

Dynamic Stretching: We're not talking about those half-assed stretches you do when you wake up in the morning. Think leg swings like you're auditioning for a Rockettes show, arm circles that could power a wind turbine and lunges that say, "I'm coming for you, pickleball!" Warm up like you mean it, or at least like you didn't just roll out of bed.

Light Cardio: Get your heart rate up with some light jogging or a few rounds of jumping jacks. Think of it as your body's way of saying, "Yes, I'm alive!" before you hit the court. Just try not to look too pleased with yourself when you're the only one who doesn't collapse after the first rally.

Sport-Specific Drills: Time to get real. Incorporate drills that mimic the actual movements you'll be making on the court. Side shuffles, short sprints, basically, all the stuff you'll be doing while pretending you know what you're doing out there. Consider it your pre-game warm-up without the shame of doing it in front of an audience.

Hydrate (Like Your Life Depends On It)

Pre-Hydrate: If you're planning to play like a beast, you better start hydrating like one. Sip that water 2-3 hours before you even think about picking up your paddle. Aim for 16-20 oz; dehydration can lead to fatigue and cramps, which are no fun. Plus, you'll have an excuse to carry around a cool water bottle.

Electrolytes: If the sun's out and you're sweating more than a liar at a polygraph test, consider throwing some electrolytes into the mix. Keep those muscles cramp-free and yourself out of the local ER.

Nutrition: Fuel Up Without Filling Up

Pre-Game Meal: About 2-3 hours before you're scheduled to destroy your opponents, eat something that fuels your game, not your nap time. Complex carbs and lean proteins, think chicken with brown rice, not that greasy burger you've been eyeing. You're here to play, not to lie down.

Snack Attack: Need a little something before you hit the court? A banana or an energy bar should do it. Just enough to keep you from passing out mid-smash, but not so much that you'll be looking for a bathroom instead of the ball.

Get Your Head In The Game

Visualization: Close your eyes and picture it: your perfect serve, your opponent's look of despair, and the crowd (okay, maybe just your friends) going wild. Visualization isn't just for the pros; it's for anyone who wants to win. So go ahead, dream big.

Focus: Clear your mind of distractions. No one cares about that email, and you can solve world peace after the game. Right now, it's all about you, your paddle, and the next point you're about to dominate.

Gear Up, Buttercup

Footwear: This isn't a fashion show, folks. It's a pickleball game. Wear shoes that'll keep you steady and supported. If you want to impress, do it with your skills, not with your choice of neon shoelaces.

Protective Gear: If you've got a history of turning your ankles into pretzels, don't be a hero. Wrap those joints up tight and keep yourself in the game instead of the hospital. The only time you should be seeing a doctor is when you're bragging about how you totally didn't need them.

Avoiding Common Injuries

Mind Your Footing (Gravity Is the Real Enemy):

Be aware of where you're stepping, especially around the kitchen area. It's easy to trip or stumble if you're not paying attention. If you take one wrong step, you could end eating court.

Pace Yourself:

Don't overdo it. If you feel tired or sore, take a break. It's better to rest than to risk an injury that could keep you off the court for weeks or, worse, give your friends something to tease you about for the rest of your life.

Safety First (Even If It's Not Cool)

Know Your Limits (And Stay Within Them):

If you have any existing health conditions, be mindful of them, and don't push yourself too hard. Listen to your body and take it easy if needed. After all, you'd rather play another day than sit on the sidelines watching everyone else have fun.

Be Aware of Others (Accidents Happen):

Always be aware of where other players are on the court. Accidents can happen if you're not paying attention, so stay alert and keep your head on a swivel unless you want to clothesline someone accidentally.

Stay Safe, Play Smart (And Keep Your Dignity Intact):

Pickleball is fun, but it's important to stay safe. With a few precautions, you can enjoy the game while minimizing the risk of injury and the embarrassment that comes with it. So play hard, but play smart, and remember that it's just a game. There's no need to die for it.

CHAPTER 12: FUN PICKLEBALL FACTS

Did You Know? (Or Are You Just Here for the Fun?)

Welcome to the chapter where you get to dazzle your friends with random pickleball trivia they didn't know they needed in their lives. Whether you're looking to win over the crowd with some obscure history or just want to drop a few fun facts between serves, this section has got you covered. From the quirky origins of the sport to the weird and wonderful world of pickleball regulations, we're diving into the fun side of pickleball that'll make you say, "Wait, seriously?" So, let's get into it. Knowing these facts might just give you the edge you need to win that next game or at least make you the most interesting person at the pickleball party.

Pickleball's Origin Story (Spoiler: It's Weird)

They say pickleball was invented in 1965 by three dads who wanted to create a fun game for their kids during the summer. They improvised with a badminton court, some paddles, and a perforated ball; the rest is history. Apparently, boredom is the mother of invention.

Why the Heck Is It Called "Pickleball"?

One theory is the game was named after the family dog, Pickles, who loved to chase the ball. Yes, you read that right. A dog named Pickles is the reason we have this glorious sport. Another theory is that it was named after the term "pickle boat," which refers to a crew made up of oarsmen left over from other boats. Either way, it's weird and wonderful.

The Fastest Growing Sport

Pickleball is one of the fastest-growing sports in the United States. It's popular with people of all ages, from kids to seniors, and it's spreading rapidly across the globe. Apparently, people have finally realized that tennis is too much work, and pickleball is the perfect compromise.

A Game for Everyone (Even Grandma)

Pickleball is so easy to learn, and fun to play, and the game has become a favorite pastime for millions of people. It's played in schools, community centers, parks, and even retirement communities. Who knew smacking a ball around could bring so many generations together?

More Fun Facts (You Need More Pickleball Trivia In Your Life)

Pickleball Paddle Regulations

According to official rules, pickleball paddles must be no longer than 17 inches and no wider than 7 inches. Regulating paddle size keeps the game fair and consistent for all players. We all know someone who'd try to bring a tennis racket if they could.

The No-Volley Zone (Aka the Kitchen)

The kitchen, or no-volley zone, was created to prevent "spiking" at the net and to encourage more strategic play. It's a unique feature that sets pickleball apart from other racquet sports and gives everyone a chance to yell, "Stay the *Bleep* out of the kitchen!" with impunity. You will see your Tennis friends struggle with this. Feel free to invite them to gain some quick wins.

The Pickleball Craze (And Why You Should Join)

Pickleball's Popularity (It's Not Just a Fad)

There are an estimated 50,000 pickleball courts across the United States, and the number keeps growing. From casual play to serious tournaments, pickleball is taking the world by storm, so you might as well jump on the bandwagon.

Join the Fun

Pickleball is more than just a game. It's a movement. Whether you're a casual player or a competitive enthusiast, you're part of a global community that's all about having fun and staying active. So grab a paddle, find a court, and see what all the fuss is about. You might just get hooked.

CHAPTER 13: HOW TO GET BETTER FAST

How to Improve Without Losing Your Sanity

So, you've been bitten by the pickleball bug, and now you're obsessed with getting better, like yesterday. But don't worry; we're here to help you level up your game without losing your mind or becoming that overly intense person no one wants to play with. Whether you're trying to finally beat that one friend who won't shut up about their "perfect serve" or just want to stop tripping over your own feet, this chapter's got your back. We're talking real tips, zero fluff, and a whole lot of laughs. Hey, if you're not having fun, what's the point? So, let's dive in before you start contemplating hiring a pickleball coach for your dog.

Play, Play, Play (Until You Can't Stand It Anymore)

The best way to get better at pickleball is simply to play as much as possible. The more you're on the court, the more you'll learn and improve, and the more you'll wonder why you didn't start playing this fabulous sport sooner.

Watch and Learn (You're Not a Pickleball Genius, Yet)

Watch experienced players and try to pick up on their techniques. Notice how they move, how they hit the ball, and how they position themselves on the court.

Then try to imitate them until you find your own style, or just steal theirs, whatever works.

Ask for Advice (And Try Not to Roll Your Eyes)

Don't be shy about asking for tips from more experienced players. Most people are happy to share their knowledge and help you improve. Just nod along, even if you're secretly thinking, "I knew that."

Practice Makes You Slightly Less Terrible

Drills (Brace Yourself for Sweat)

Practice specific shots like serves, dinks, and volleys. Set up targets and try to hit them consistently. Repetition builds muscle memory and confidence, and maybe that smaller pants size you've been waiting to get into.

Play with Different Opponents (So You Don't Get Cocky)

Challenge yourself by playing with a variety of partners and opponents. Different playing styles will push you to adapt and grow your skills and keep you from getting too comfortable.

Stay Motivated (Even If You're Having A Bad Hair Day)

Set Goals (Showing Up Is a Goal)

Whether it's improving your serve, mastering the

kitchen, or winning a local tournament, set goals for yourself and work towards them. Just make sure they're realistic. No one likes a dreamer who's always disappointed.

Celebrate Progress (Even If It's Tiny)

Recognize and celebrate your improvements, no matter how small. Every step forward is a victory or a reason to treat yourself to something nice.

Have Fun Along the Way (What Else Are You Going to Do?)

Remember, the journey to improvement is just as important as the destination. Enjoy the process, keep a positive attitude, and have fun as you work on becoming the best pickleball player you can be. Or at least a player who doesn't embarrass themselves too often.

CHAPTER 14: POST- GAME REVOVERY: STRETCH, BRAG, AND PLOT YOUR NEXT VICTORY

How to Recover Like a Pickleball Pro

You've just crushed it on the pickleball court. Well, maybe you didn't crush it, but you survived, and that's worth celebrating. Now it's time to recover like a pro, which means stretching out those muscles, bragging about your epic (or not-so-epic) game, and, of course, plotting how you're going to destroy your opponents next time. This chapter is your guide to postgame glory, from the perfect cool-down to the art of humble bragging. Half the fun of playing is talking about it afterward. So grab that protein shake (or, let's be real, a beer), and let's make sure you're ready to hit the court again without limping like you just spent hours scrolling through funny pickleball memes and forgot how to stand.

Cool Down (So You Don't Feel Like Used Punching Bag Tomorrow)

After the game, take a few minutes to cool down. Do some light stretching to help your muscles recover and prevent soreness. Focus on your legs, arms, and back; nothing ruins your day faster than not being able to move.

Hydrate (Like You've Been Lost in the Desert)

Rehydrate by drinking plenty of water. If you've had a particularly intense game, consider a sports drink to replenish electrolytes, or just stick with water if you're not into that neon-colored stuff.

Reflect on the Game (Or Just Gloat)

Take a moment to think about how you played. What went well? What could you improve next time? Reflection is key to getting better, or just spend a few minutes gloating if you won.

Social Time (Who Doesn't Love A Post-Game Hangout?)

Celebrate with Friends

Whether you won or lost, celebrate with your fellow players. Grab a bite to eat, have a drink, or just hang out and chat. The social aspect of pickleball is one of its best features. Plus, it's a great excuse to avoid going home just yet.

Share Highlights (And Low Points)

Talk about the highlights of the game, great shots, funny moments, and epic rallies. Reliving the game is half the fun. Plus, it's a good way to remind everyone of your brilliance (or their mistakes).

Planning For Next Time

Schedule Your Next Game (So No One Can Weasel Out)

While the excitement is still fresh, set a date for your next game. Consistent play is the best way to keep improving and having fun and to make sure everyone stays hooked on pickleball.

Stay Connected (So They Don't Forget You)

Keep in touch with your pickleball friends through a group chat or a local club. Being proactive at staying connected helps maintain camaraderie and keeps everyone motivated to play. Plus, it's a great way to share memes and trash talk.

Enjoy the Afterglow (You Earned It)

There's nothing like the satisfaction of a good game of pickleball. Whether you're basking in a win or reflecting on a loss, take pride in the fact that you're out there playing, improving, and having a blast. And if all else fails, at least you got some exercise, right?

CHAPTER 15: JOINING A PICKLEBALL COMMUNITY

How to Find Your Pickleball People (And Not Scare Them Off)

Now, you're ready to find your crew, the fellow paddle-wielding warriors who share your obsession. But how do you join the pickleball community without coming across like a desperate newbie or, worse, a total weirdo? Fear not. We'll show you how to slide into the pickleball scene like a seasoned pro, make friends without scaring them off, and maybe even snag an invite to that elusive weekend pickleball brunch. Whether you're looking for casual games or die-hard competition, we'll help you find your people and fit in like you've been dinking with them for years. So, let's dive in and get you mingling without creeping anyone out.

Local Clubs (Make New Friends)

Many communities have pickleball clubs that welcome players of all levels. Joining a club is a great way to meet new people, find regular playing partners, get involved in local tournaments, or just have someone to complain to about your backhand.

Community Centers (It's Not Just for Seniors)

Check your local community center or parks department for pickleball leagues and open play times. These are often casual and open to everyone, so you probably don't have to worry about being the worst player there.

Online Groups (For the Socially Awkward)

Join online pickleball communities on social media platforms. These groups are great for sharing tips, finding games, and connecting with players from all over without having to make eye contact.

Making Connections (Without Being A Creep)

Be Friendly (But Not Too Friendly)

Don't be afraid to introduce yourself to other players. Pickleball is a social sport, and most people are more than happy to welcome new players; they just don't come on too strong. Yes, looking up someone's address and randomly driving past their house to see if they are at the court is creepy. Be cool.

Get Involved

Participate in events, volunteer to help with tournaments, or simply show up regularly. The more involved you are, the more connected you'll feel, and the more likely people will remember your name.

Building New Friendships

Play Regularly (So They Can't Forget You)

The more you play with others, the stronger your connections will become. Regular games lead to friendships that extend beyond the court and maybe give you someone to grab a drink with afterward.

Socialize Off the Court (It's Not All About Pickleball, Right?)

Invite your pickleball friends to social gatherings or meet up outside of game times. Socializing off the court helps build a deeper sense of community and strengthens friendships, or as a fallback, it gives you something to do on weekends.

The Power Of Community

Support and Encouragement (We All Need It)

A pickleball community provides support, encouragement, and motivation to keep playing and improving. You're never alone when you're part of a team, even if that team is just a bunch of people who like to hit a ball around.

A Shared Passion (Obsession)

There's something special about connecting with others who share your passion for pickleball. It's more than just a game. Pickleball is a way to connect with others on a deeper level and potentially a way to avoid awkward small talk.

Get Involved, Stay Connected (Or Risk FOMO)

Pickleball isn't just a game; it's a movement, a social network, and a full-blown obsession—kind of like your aunt's relentless matchmaking, but way more fun. Being part of a pickleball community means more than just hitting that perfect shot; it revolves around building connections, sharing laughs, and cheering each other on. Don't be that lone wolf howling at the moon—find your pack, join the revolution, and experience the joy of the game with people who get it. Because, let's be real, nothing's worse than missing out on the camaraderie and epic inside jokes that make this sport so addictive.

CHAPTER 16: WHY PICKLEBALL IS HERE TO STAY

Why Pickleball Isn't Going Anywhere

You thought pickleball was just a passing fad, like fidget spinners or avocado toast. But here you are, paddle in hand, trying to explain to your friends why you'd rather dink than do just about anything else. The truth is, pickleball has officially taken over, and it's not going anywhere, just like you, glued to the court, chasing that next addictive rally. In this chapter, we'll break down why this sport has the staying power of your Aunt Martha's fruitcake at Christmas and why you're destined to keep playing until your knees give out (or they pry that paddle from your cold, overworked hand). So sit back, embrace your new reality, and get comfortable. Pickleball is here to stay, and you might as well make the most of it.

A Game for All Ages (And All Fitness Levels)

One of the reasons pickleball has become so popular is its appeal to players of all ages. From kids to seniors, everyone can enjoy this sport. Its ease of learning and low impact make it accessible to all, even if you haven't exercised since the Clinton administration.

Social and Fun (Like Tennis, but Without the Elitism)

Pickleball thrives on its blend of friendly competition and community spirit. Unlike some sports that carry an air of exclusivity, pickleball is all about being welcoming and inclusive. It's become a go-to for people who want to stay active, make new friends, or just find a fun way to escape the house and show off their paddle skills (and maybe kick some butt while they're at it).

Growing Popularity (Everyone Finally Realized a Wiffle Ball Version of Tennis Is Awesome)

Pickleball courts are popping up everywhere, from public parks to private clubs. The sport's rapid growth shows no signs of slowing down as more and more people discover the joy of pickleball and the pain of trying to explain it to their friends.

Why It's So Addictive

Easy to Learn, Hard to Master (So You'll Never Get Bored)

While it's easy to pick up the basics, pickleball offers endless opportunities for skill development. This keeps the game challenging and engaging, no matter how long you've been playing or how badly you suck.

Quick Games (So You Can Play Without Ditching Your Responsibilities)

Games are short and sweet, making it easy to fit into your day. Whether you have 15 minutes or an hour, there's always time for a quick game of pickleball and a quick break from reality.

A Sport For All Ages And Stages Of Life

(And It's Cheaper Than Golf)

Low Impact (So You Won't End Up in Physical Therapy)

Pickleball is gentler on the joints compared to other sports like tennis. Even retired tennis legends have come forward, sharing how pickleball is a sport they can continue playing (kicking butts and taking names) for many years. Get off the couch and start unleashing your inner pickleball spirit that is active and healthy. Should all else fail, it will give you an excuse to wear sporty clothes.

Lifelong and Generational Enjoyment

The blend of physical activity, mental challenge, and social interaction makes pickleball a sport that people stick with for life and share across generations of family–from the sticky youngsters to the smelly uncle nobody wants to sit next to during the holidays.

The Future Of Pickleball

Expanding Globally (Spread the Love - It's the Pickle Way)

While pickleball started in the United States, it's rapidly gaining popularity worldwide. More countries are embracing the sport, and international competitions are on the rise. Apparently, the world needs to argue about another sport.

Inclusion in Schools

Schools are beginning to introduce pickleball to students as part of their physical education programs, ensuring the next generation of players is ready to carry the torch and the next generation of P.E. the teacher is ready to coach. The sky's the limit! Let's support this as an official Olympic sport!

Pickleball Is Here to Stay (So Get Used to It)

The growth of pickleball shows no signs of slowing down. As more people discover the sport's joy, community, and health benefits, pickleball is poised to become a global favorite for generations to come. Until then, grab a paddle and join the fun!

CHAPTER 17: FREQUENTLY ASKED QUESTIONS & CONFUSIONS

FAQs About Pickleball (Because We All Have Dumb Questions)

No one comes out of the womb knowing the ins and outs of pickleball. Instead, we've got ALL the questions. Dumb questions. Questions that make you wonder if maybe you should've taken up knitting instead. But don't worry! This chapter is your safe space, where you can ask all those burning pickleball questions without fear of judgment, well, maybe just a little judgment. From "What the heck is a 'dink'?" to "Why is it called pickleball, and does it involve actual pickles?" we've got you covered. Consider this your cheat sheet to understand the game so you can finally stop pretending to know what you're doing.

Is pickleball hard to learn?

Answer: Not at all! Pickleball is designed to be easy to learn and fun to play. Most people pick up the basics faster than they can Google "pickleball." If you're struggling, don't worry; you're probably just overthinking it. And hey, that's why you're reading this book, right? Give it a few games, and you'll be the one rolling your eyes at new players in no time.

How long does a typical game last?

Answer: A typical game of pickleball lasts between 15 and 30 minutes, depending on the skill level of the players and how much time you spend talking smack. Games are usually played to 11 points, and you must win by 2. So, whether you've got 20 minutes between meetings or a whole afternoon to kill, pickleball fits perfectly into your schedule. Plus, it's way more fun than whatever else you were going to do.

Do I need any special training to play?

Answer: No special training is required! Just grab a paddle or a ball and start playing. Pickleball is accessible to everyone, and the best way to improve is simply by playing regularly. If you're still nervous, just remember: everyone else was a beginner at one point in time.

What's the best way to improve my game?

Answer: The best way to improve is to play as often as you can. Practice different shots, work on your footwork, and play with a variety of partners and opponents to challenge yourself. Watching experienced players and asking for tips can also help you learn faster; just don't annoy them too much.

Can kids play pickleball?

Answer: Of course! Pickleball is great for all ages; kids can pick it up quickly. It's a fun and safe way to get the whole family moving together or to get the kids off their damn screens for once. Just be prepared for them to beat you eventually. It's a fair exchange since children are great ball chasers.

Can pickleball really help me get fit?

Answer: You bet! Pickleball is sneaky. While you're busy having fun, it's secretly getting you in shape. The mix of short sprints, quick reflexes, and arm swings gives you a full-body workout without making you feel like you're doing one. So yes, it's a legit way to burn calories, improve your cardio, and maybe even shed a few pounds; just don't expect to get ripped overnight. Unless you're playing against a banger, then you might be running a lot more than you planned.

Should I be worried about "Pickleball Elbow"?:

Answer: Pickleball elbow is a real thing, similar to tennis elbow, and it can happen if you play too much or have poor technique. The key to avoiding it is to warm up properly, use good form, and not overdo it. And if you start feeling pain, take a break, stretch, and maybe ice it down. After all, it's hard to show off your skills if you're sidelined with an injury. Play smart, and you'll stay in the game.

Top Rules In Question: The Ones You'll Argue About (And Probably Lose)

Can I step into the kitchen anytime?

Answer: Step out of the kitchen (the non-volley zone) unless the ball has bounced there first. The kitchen rule is designed to prevent players from standing too close to the net and dominating with volleys. Remember, you can step into the kitchen after the ball bounces but can't volley from there. If you do, prepare for the collective groan of everyone else on the court.

What if the ball lands on the line?

Answer: If the ball lands on any part of the line, it's considered "in." All lines on the court fall under this, including the baseline, sidelines, and kitchen line (except, of course, on a serve). So, if the ball touches the line, keep playing! And if your opponent argues, just hand them this book and refer to this chapter.

Do I have to switch sides during the game?

Answer: Yes, you and your partner will switch sides in doubles after your team scores each point. This helps balance any advantages that one side of the court might have, such as wind or sun, or just to keep you from getting too comfortable.

What happens if the ball hits the net on a serve?

Answer: If the ball hits the net but still lands in the correct service box, it's called a "let," and you get to serve again without penalty. If the serve doesn't land in the correct box after hitting the net, it's considered a fault, and you lose your serve. Don't worry; it happens to everyone. Just try not to do it too often.

Can I play pickleball indoors?

Answer: Absolutely! Pickleball can be played indoors or outdoors. Many gyms, community centers, and sports complexes have indoor pickleball courts. Just ensure you're using the right type of ball for the surface you're playing on. Indoor balls are typically lighter and have fewer holes than outdoor balls. We don't recommend playing in your mom's living room or where windows or decor can be smashed.

CHAPTER 18: TRADING TENNIS WHITES FOR PICKLEBALL SMILES

How to Transition Without Losing Your Cool

(or Your Friends)

So, you've spent years perfecting that oh-so-smooth tennis backhand, flaunting those crisp whites like you're playing on the grass courts of London and throwing in a few grunts that would make any professional tennis player proud. But now, you're sneaking glances at the pickleball court with a mix of curiosity and, let's be honest, a bit of snobby side-eye. Don't worry, tennis snob (we were once like you)! You can make the leap to pickleball without losing your cool or your tennis posse. Who knows, you might even (get ready to clutch your pearls) enjoy yourself.

Embrace Both Worlds (Why the Heck Not?)

Here's the deal: you don't have to choose. Switching to pickleball doesn't mean you're betraying tennis. Start dabbling in both, and suddenly, you're the MVP of all racquet sports. Pickleball can be your fun, social alternative when you're not in the mood to sprint across a massive court. Plus, those tennis skills? They give you a head start in pickleball; just remember, you're not here to channel your inner tennis warrior. The trick to keeping your tennis friends happy? Don't ditch them. Keep playing both because variety is the spice of life, and you, my friend, can have it all. And by "all," I mean the ability to dominate two courts while still looking like a snack.

Bonus: You Can Still Look Fabulous (Just Leave the Snobbery at the Door)

Good news: You've dropped serious cash on all that tennis gear. Totally pickleball-appropriate. You'll be the best-dressed player on the court, hands down. But while your outfit might scream, "I'm ready for Centre Court or to take a tea with the Queen," your attitude should say, "I'm here to have a blast." Strut your stuff, but check the tennis snobbery at the gate. Pickleball is about fun, community, and letting your hair down, literally and figuratively. So, toss on that headband, flash that winning smile, and remember: nobody cares if your shoes match your paddle as long as you're bringing the good vibes.

Similarities to Tennis (But Less Running and More Fun)

Are you worried about losing your competitive edge? Don't be. For non-pros, pickleball is like tennis's cooler, more laid-back cousin. You've got serving, volleying, and strategic shot placement, just on a smaller court with a lighter ball. Translation? Less running, more fun. And did we mention it's easier on your knees? Yeah, you'll adapt in no time, especially when you realize you don't need a standing appointment with your massage therapist after every game. Plus, the only thing better than beating your friends at tennis is also beating them at pickleball. Double the victory, double the satisfaction.

Keep All Your Friends (No One Wants to Be a Lone Wolf)

There is no need to abandon your tennis friends; instead, bring them along for the ride. Organize "Tennis vs. Pickleball" events, and let your pals enjoy the best of both worlds. They'll thank you for it or at least tolerate you a little more. Worried about tennis treason? Relax. Pickleball isn't a betrayal; it's just another way to have fun. And who couldn't use a little more of that? Plus, you'll get to enjoy the sweet sound of tennis players eating humble pie when they realize pickleball isn't just for retirees. It's a whole new way to show off.

Celebrate the Best of Both Worlds (So No One Feels Left Out)

Every sport has its charms. Tennis gives you tradition and a great workout, while pickleball offers a social vibe and a lot less stress. Why choose? Enjoy both for what they are. And if your tennis friends are still on the fence, remind them that pickleball is perfect for those days when they're not up for a full-on tennis match. Balance is key, my friend, both on the court and in life. So, whether you're sweating it out on the tennis court or laughing it up in pickleball, you're winning at life (and probably the match).

Be the Bridge, It's Better Than Burning Them

Be the hero who introduces your tennis crew to pickleball and vice versa. You'll expand your circle, deepen your connections, and always have someone to play with, no matter which sport you're in the mood for. You really can have it all: tennis racket in one hand, pickleball paddle in the other. Now, go out there and dominate both courts like the multi-talented sports star you are. And when your friends ask how you do it, just smile and say, "What can I say? I'm just that good." Now head to the court and show them how it's done!

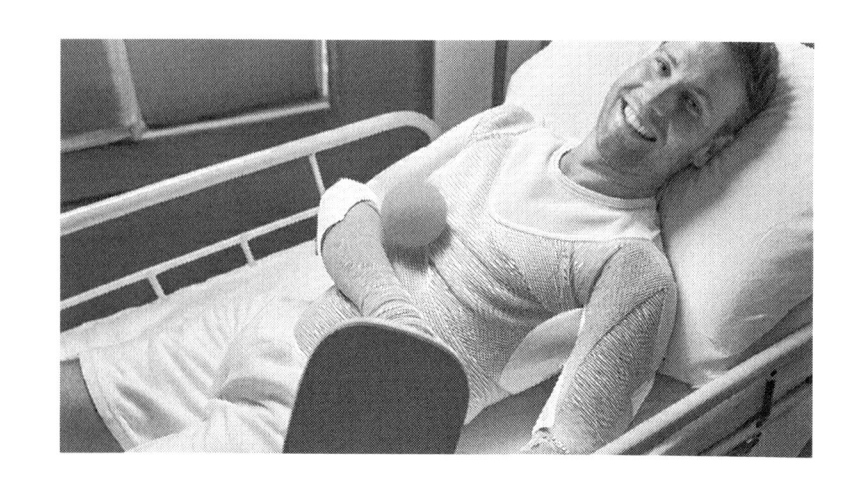

CHAPTER 19: PICKLEBALL OUCHIES: LAUGH, CRY, AND SHAKE IT OFF

Bragging Through the Pain (Wear That Injury

Like a Medal of Honor)

Pickleball ouchie? Wear that pain with pride. Your injury is your new best pickleball story. We say, strut that injury like it's the latest fashion statement.

We interrupt this book with legal talk again: Pickleball injuries are all fun and games until you're explaining to your doctor how you pulled a hamstring trying to win a point—so, enjoy the laughs but play smart. For any health-related concerns, please consult a doctor before attempting to out-smash your competition.

Okay, now that that is covered, here's your guide to treating common pickleball injuries with just the right amount of humor and self-deprecation.

The Paddle Wrist

Diagnosis: You've been swinging that paddle like a hammer, and now your wrist is plotting revenge.

Treatment: Drop the paddle and back away slowly. Nobody's impressed by a serve that looks like you're auditioning for a mime troupe. Ice it, wrap it, and soak up those sympathy points. Bonus tip: Remember, finesse beats force. Save the super moves for smashing avocados.

The Pickleball Tango

Diagnosis: You went for that impossible shot and ended up in a dance with gravity and lost.

Treatment: Brush yourself off, take a dramatic bow, and then stretch like your dignity depends on it. Let's be honest, it does. And hey, at least you tried, which is more than most people can say about their dance moves.

The Net Tangle

Diagnosis: You and the net had a little too much enthusiasm, resulting in an unplanned wrestling match.

Treatment: Give the net a firm handshake and apologize for the roughhousing. Then, hydrate, stretch, and remember: this isn't wrestling; keep the drama on the scoreboard, not the net.

The Pickleball Elbow

Diagnosis: It's like tennis elbow, but with fewer sponsorship deals and more "should've known better" vibes.

Treatment: Rest it, ice it, and wear that brace like it's the latest accessory. And maybe, just maybe, consider dialing down the power shots. You do not have to obliterate the ball to win. Placing it just right, like decorating a cake, will get you to victory. You could also just bake a cake and bring it to the next game; delicious food bribery also works.

The Footwork Fumble

Diagnosis: You tripped over your feet because, clearly, coordination is just a suggestion.

Treatment: Besides working on your footwork (seriously, though), laugh it off. At least you're out there giving it your all, unlike those couch potatoes. And next time, remember where your feet are supposed to go. You've got this!

The Giggle Strain

Diagnosis: You laughed so hard at the latest pickleball mishap that now your sides ache.

Treatment: Absolutely no treatment is required; this is the good kind of pain. Keep laughing! As we've said before, if pickleball isn't making you smile, you're doing it wrong. Just maybe tone it down a notch if you're laughing at your partner. Or don't, your call.

Laugh It Off (What Else Are You Going To Do?)

In the grand scheme of things, pickleball injuries are usually minor and always come with a great story. The best cure? A positive attitude, a little rest, and a lot of laughs. So, play hard, take care of yourself, and always find the humor in those "oops" moments. Remember, it's not a real game until someone walks away with a new bruise and a story to match.

pickleball
{pik-uhl-bawl}
noun
1. Like tennis, but fun

CHAPTER 20: THE PICKLEBALL GLOSSARY: 'DINK' ISN'T JUST A WEIRD NOISE

Speak Pickleball Like a Pro: The Lingo You Didn't

Know You Needed

Say what? From dinks to smashes, Berts and Ernes (pronounced ER-nee - yes, like your favorite childhood puppets), bangers, and the ever-mysterious kitchen, we've got you covered on translating all top pickleball lingo. So, before you hit the court and start throwing around words you barely understand, take a moment to brush up on the essentials. Trust us, knowing the difference between a "fault" and a "foot fault" might just save you from some embarrassing moments and give you a few laughs along the way.

Dink *(noun)*
It's a soft, strategic shot that barely clears the net and lands in the kitchen (no, not your actual kitchen, but more on that later).

Usage: "Dink, dink, dink… and now my opponent is ready to throw their paddle."

Kitchen *(noun)*
The no-volley zone is a 7-foot area on either side of the net where you are absolutely forbidden to smash the ball. If you do, prepare for some serious side-eye.

Usage: "Stay the *bleep* out of the kitchen unless you're making snacks."

Third Shot Drop (*noun*)
The holy grail of pickleball shots. It's the shot pros say you need to master, but for most of us, it's the one we try to pull off and end up dropping the ball into the net instead.

Usage: "My third shot drop is more of a third shot flop."

Pickled (*adjective*)
Losing a game without scoring a single point. Ouch.

Usage: "We got pickled, and now we're pickled. Let's go drown our sorrows in actual pickles."

Erne (*noun*)
A daring, sideways leap over the kitchen to volley the ball right at your opponent's feet. Attempt with caution unless you have ninja-like reflexes (or a death wish).

Usage: "Did you see that Erne? No? Me neither because it was so damn fast."

Lob (*noun*)
A high, arching shot aimed at the back of the court. Great for making your opponent run like they've got somewhere to be.

Usage: "Lob it high and watch them scramble… unless they smash it back, then, uh, run."

Fault (*noun*)

STAY THE BLEEP OUT OF THE KITCHEN

A fancy way of saying, "Oops, you messed up." Faults could be stepping into the kitchen during a volley, serving out of bounds, or any other pickleball blunder.

Usage: "Fault! Again! Maybe I should read the rulebook– Nah."

Smash *(noun)*
The exhilarating act of slamming the ball down into your opponent's side of the court. Best done with a loud grunt for added drama.

Usage: "I smashed that ball so hard it's now reconsidering its life choices."

Volley *(noun)*
Hitting the ball before it bounces. Usually followed by your partner yelling, "Stay out of the kitchen!"
Usage: "I love a good volley, just not when I accidentally step into the kitchen and lose the point."

Banger *(noun)*
A player who hits every shot as hard as possible, whether it's necessary or not. Subtlety? Nah, they wouldn't dare.

Usage: "The Banger strikes again. Can someone please tell them this isn't tennis?"

Paddle *(noun)*
The essential tool for pickleball. It can be wooden,

composite, or carbon fiber. Either way, it's what you'll use to make (or break) your game.

Usage: "It's not the size paddle; it's how you use it. But seriously, this new paddle is amazing."

Doubles *(noun)*
A game format where two players team up against another pair. Great for camaraderie, but be warned: you might end up arguing with your partner more than your opponents.

Usage: "Doubles is fun, but it's also a great way to find out who your real friends are."

Singles *(noun)*
A one-on-one battle of skill, speed, and endurance. Also known as "the quickest way to realize you need to work on your cardio."

Usage: "Singles is where legends are made, or where I get winded in 30 seconds."

Pickleball Addict *(noun)*
Someone who can't go a day without playing pickleball, thinking about pickleball, or talking about pickleball. If you're reading this glossary, you might be one.

Usage: "Hi, my name is [Your Name], and I'm a pickleball addict."

Pickleball Junkie *(noun)*

The next level of addiction. You're not just playing; and you're living, breathing, and evangelizing pickleball to anyone who will listen.

Usage: "I've become a pickleball junkie. I'm thinking of starting a pickleball-themed restaurant."

Foot Fault *(noun)*
The act of stepping on or over the baseline during a serve or stepping into the kitchen during a volley. Not to be confused with a dance move.

Usage: "Foot fault? More like foot fail."

Let *(noun)*
When the ball touches the net on a serve and lands in the correct service court, it's a do-over, not a get-out-of-jail-free card.

Usage: "Let's do that serve again, see what I did there?"

Paddle Tap *(noun)*
The pickleball equivalent of a handshake. A quick tap of the paddles to say "good game" without actually having to touch another human.

Usage: "Paddle tap? Or are we too competitive for that?"

Pickleball Court *(noun)*
The sacred ground where all the action happens. It's smaller than a tennis court but filled with ten times the drama.

Usage: "Meet me on the pickleball court. Things are about to get real."

Serve and Slice *(noun)*
When you serve the ball with a side spin that makes it dance all over the court like it's had one too many.

Usage: "That serve and slice had my opponent doing the cha-cha."

The Noob Serve *(noun)*
The first-time serve that barely makes it over the net or doesn't. Hey, everyone starts somewhere.

Usage: "My noob serve game is strong today. I swear I'll get better, maybe."

Kitchen Creep *(noun)*
The sneaky habit of edging closer to the kitchen line during a rally. Careful, get caught, and it's all over.

Usage: "Watch that kitchen creep! Unless you want to hand over the point."

Pickleball Swagger *(noun)*
The unmistakable strut of someone who just nailed a shot they didn't even know they could pull off.

Usage: "Check out that pickleball swagger. Too bad it's the first point they've won all day."

Sizzle Shot *(noun)*

A shot so hot it practically leaves a trail of smoke as it flies past your opponent.

Usage: "That sizzle shot was so fire, I'm surprised it didn't set off alarms."

You are now fluent in the art of pickleball speak! With these terms in your back pocket, you'll be dropping dinks and dodging foot faults like a pro—or at least talking like one. So go forth, sprinkle some pickleball lingo into your life, and watch your friends' eyes glaze over with awe (or confusion, but hey, same thing). Just remember, if you start using "kitchen creep" in actual conversations, it might be time to admit you're a full-blown pickleball addict. Now, get out there and serve up some sass with that new vocabulary of yours!

CHAPTER 21: GET OUT AND PLAY!

*Ready to Hit the Court?
(You've Got This!)*

Now that you know the rules, strategies, and tips for playing pickleball, it's time to get out on the court and put them into practice. The more you play, the more you'll improve, and the more you'll annoy your friends by constantly talking about it.

Don't Wait (There's No Time Like the Present)

Whether you're playing with friends and family or joining a local group, the most important thing is to get out there and start playing. Pickleball is a game that's best learned by doing, so jump in and enjoy the experience. And if you mess up, just blame it on the wind.

Tips For Getting Out There

Invite Friends (Misery Loves Company)

The more, the merrier! Invite your friends or family to join you for a game. The social aspect of pickleball is one of its biggest draws, so don't hesitate to share the fun. Plus, it's always more fun to beat people you know.

Set Small Goals (You're Not a Pickleball Pro, Yet)

Whether it's mastering your serve, improving your dinks, or playing in your first tournament, set small goals to keep yourself motivated and excited about the game. And if you reach them, reward yourself with something nice, like a new paddle or a pizza.

Enjoy The Journey

Every Game is a Learning Experience (Or a Humbling

One)

Win or lose, every game you play is an opportunity to learn and improve. Keep a positive attitude, and remember that the most important thing is to have fun unless you're a sore loser, in which case, maybe this isn't the sport (or book) for you.

Celebrate Your Progress (You're a Pickleball God Now)

As you continue playing, take time to celebrate your progress. Whether it's hitting a new milestone or simply having a great time with friends, recognize and enjoy the moments; they're all you've got.

The Pickleball Adventure (Or an Opportunity to Trash Talk)

Your pickleball journey is just beginning. Whether you become a casual player or a competitive enthusiast, the most important thing is to enjoy the ride. So grab your paddle, head to the court, and start shaking what your momma gave ya.

Pass It Along (Sharing Is Caring)

Share the Love

Now that you've learned the ins and outs of pickleball, it's time to spread the joy. Share this book with friends, family, and anyone who might be interested in learning the game. The more people who play, the more fun it gets, and the more people you can beat.

Be an Ambassador

By introducing others to pickleball, you're helping to grow the sport and create a welcoming, active community. Whether you're organizing a neighborhood game, convincing your cousin to give it a try, or just leaving this book conspicuously on a park bench, you're helping to make the world a better place, one paddle at a time. Who wouldn't want to be responsible for sparking the next great pickleball rivalry?

Pay It Forward

Pickleball is all about community and connection. By passing along this book and encouraging others to play, you're helping to build a positive, inclusive environment where everyone can join the Paddle Posh mission to empower play and inspire confidence on and off the pickleball court.

#poshitivity

PADDLE POSH

CONGRATULATIONS, YOU'VE MADE IT THROUGH THE BOOK!

By now, you should be well-equipped to hit the pickleball court with confidence, humor, and just enough irreverence to keep things interesting. Whether you're playing for fun, competing with friends, or just trying to avoid the dreaded kitchen faults, remember that the most important rule of all is to enjoy yourself.

Pickleball is more than just a game. It's a way to connect, laugh, and maybe even break a sweat without taking life too seriously. The court is your playground, and whether you're a seasoned pro or a newbie still figuring out which end of the paddle to hold, there's always something new to learn and enjoy.

So go out there, invite your friends and family, and show them why pickleball is the best thing since sliced bread. Just remember:

1. ***Stay the Bleep Out of the Kitchen*** – because rules are rules, and nobody likes a fault.
2. **Laugh at Your Mistakes** – because we all make them, and it's way more fun that way.
3. **Keep Playing, Keep Learning** – because there's always room for improvement, and besides, it's a blast.

Thanks for sticking with us through this book. Now, grab your paddle, hit the court, and most importantly, **have a damn good time**.

See you on the court!
—The Pickleball Enthusiasts Who Wrote This Book

ABOUT THE PADDLE POSH TEAM

The Paddle Posh Team is a collective of passionate pickleball enthusiasts dedicated to bringing a fresh, fun, and fabulously posh perspective to the world of pickleball. As the brains behind Paddle Posh, they've combined their love for the game with a knack for humor and style, crafting content that's as entertaining as it is informative.

Visit www.paddleposh.com, where we serve up more pickleball gold, such as game-changing tips, insider tricks, and the kind of pickleball wisdom that'll have you owning the court, looking hot, and cracking up your friends.

Our Mission: We're not just here to teach you the rules of pickleball in a satirical and witty way. We're here to make sure you enjoy every minute of it, both on and off the court. Our goal is to empower players of all levels to feel confident, look good, and have a damn good time while playing the sport we all love.

Our Team: Comprising seasoned players, coaches, and just a few folks who are really good at making people laugh, the Paddle Posh Team brings a unique blend of expertise and wit to everything we do. From writing books that make you snort with laughter to curating top-tier gear that makes you feel like a champion, we're committed to elevating the pickleball experience.

Why We Wrote This Book: We believe pickleball should be accessible, enjoyable, and just a little bit irreverent. That's why we created this book: to give you the tools, tips, and tricks you need to play your best game, all while keeping things light-hearted and fun. Whether you're a newbie or a seasoned pro, our goal is to make sure you leave the court with a smile (and maybe a few less bruises).

Join Us: If you love pickleball, a good laugh, and a touch of class, you're in the right place. The Paddle Posh Team is here to guide you, entertain you, and, most importantly, remind you to stay out of the kitchen. We're redefining what it means to play pickleball, one witty remark, and stylish serve at a time.

PADDLE POSH

FOR THE LOVE OF PICKLEBALL, SHARE THIS BOOK

Who else could seriously benefit from this book? Maybe they're new to pickleball, and maybe they still think staying out of the kitchen is cooking advice, or maybe they need to lighten up with some laughs. Either way, when you're done soaking up all this pickleball brilliance, don't keep it to yourself. Make a list of those who could use a good laugh (and a lesson), and pass this book along, or casually drop the title like you're doing them the biggest favor of their lives. Because, let's face it, pickleball is way more fun when everyone is winning (and having fun). So go ahead, pay it forward— one paddle blunder at a time.

Made in the USA
Columbia, SC
22 November 2024